How To Embarrass Your Kids
Without Even Trying

By Joan Holleman & Audrey Sherins

Illustrated by Stephen Carpenter

 Meadowbrook Press
Distributed by Simon & Schuster
New York

This book would not have been possible without our seven wonderful children (some of whom have children of their own). We thank them all for the opportunity of being their parents, a joy that increases with each passing day.

Joan's brood includes Bob Doviak, Cathy Doviak Mahmud, Elizabeth Doviak, and Abigail Holleman.

Audrey's offspring are Lisa Sherins Robbins, Dana Sherins, and Mara Nicole Sherins.

Library of Congress Cataloging-in-Publication Data

Holleman, Joan.
    How to embarrass your kids without even trying / by Joan Holleman
 & Audrey Sherins; illustrated by Stephen Carpenter.
        p.   cm.
    ISBN 0-88166-194-5
    1.   Adolescence—Humor. 2.   Parenting—Humor. I.   Sherins, Audrey.
 II.   Title.
 PN6231.A26H65   1992
 818' .540208—dc20   92-27613
                                                                          CIP

Simon & Schuster Ordering # 0-671-79203-2

Published by Meadowbrook Press, 18318 Minnetonka Boulevard, Deephaven, Minnesota 55391.

BOOK TRADE DISTRIBUTION by Simon & Schuster, a division of Simon and Schuster, Inc., 1230 Avenue of the Americas, New York, NY 10020.

Editor: Bruce Lansky
Editorial Coordinator: Jay Johnson
Desktop Coordinator: Jon C. Wright
Art Director: Tabor Harlow
Production Coordinator: Matthew Thurber
Cover and Interior Artwork: Stephen Carpenter

    93 94 95 96 97   6 5 4 3

Printed in the United States of America

CONTENTS

INTRODUCTION

Who doesn't remember the pain of adolescence? Who
can forget the low self-esteem, the bubbling hormones, the
obsessive self-consciousness, the unpredictable mood
swings? Between the charm of childhood and the promise
of maturity lies the murky abyss of the preteen and teen
years, where embarrassment and humiliation are constant
threats.

How to Embarrass Your Kids Without Even Trying is a
tongue-in-cheek look at the numerous ways in which
parents unwittingly embarrass their children and add to
the stress of growing up. Humor is a great tonic for getting
through any of life's difficulties, and we have found a funny
side to many of our experiences with our own teens. We
hope you'll laugh along with us as you see your family
reflected here!

Dress up like Frankenstein and try to scare Halloweeners.

CELEBRATIONS

Wear a bow tie with blinking lights to welcome in the
New Year.

◆

Get tipsy after you drink champagne on New Year's Eve.

◆

Pinch people who aren't wearing green on
St. Patrick's Day.

◆

Put some dog biscuits in your child's bag lunch on
April Fool's Day.

◆

Safety-pin your child's sandwich together for another
April Fool's Day laugh.

◆

Be the only one on your street to fly a flag on Flag Day.

Be the only one on your street *not* to fly a flag on Flag Day.

◆

Have your illegal fireworks confiscated on the Fourth of July.

◆

Set off the neighbor's smoke alarm with your Labor Day barbecue.

◆

Welcome trick or treaters in the Superman costume you wore to your Halloween frat party.

◆

Hand out toothbrushes and toothpaste as treats.

◆

Wear pilgrim garb for Thanksgiving.

◆

Announce to the twenty-two people at Thanksgiving dinner that your teen has a special friend.

◆

Kiss your spouse under the mistletoe.

◆

Kiss anyone under the mistletoe.

Suggest that your teen stand under the mistletoe.

◆

Kiss your teen's date under the mistletoe.

◆

Ask the waiters to sing "Happy Birthday!" to your teen at a crowded restaurant.

◆

Be sure the birthday cake has relighting candles.

Make your daughter wear your first knitting project, even
though it's two sizes too small.

YOU LOOK
MAHVELOUS, DAHLING!

Dress like your kids.

◆

Dress like your parents.

◆

Wear your old clothes.

◆

Wear the latest fashions.

◆

Join a local nudist colony.

◆

Buy matching outfits for your family trip to Disney World.

Rent Victorian costumes for your family Christmas card photo.

◆

Wear your high-waters to the PTA fair.

◆

Wear your old bell-bottoms to the father/son baseball game.

◆

Have fingernails long enough to rival the Guinness record.

◆

Bite your fingernails.

◆

Have grease under your fingernails.

◆

Make your son wear Grandpa's old tuxedo to the prom.

◆

Make your teen wear your hand-me-down polyester shirts and other '70s fashions.

◆

Pick lint off your teen's clothes in public.

Wear sandals with socks.

◆

Make a necklace out of your teens' baby teeth.

◆

Sport stiletto heels and fishnet hose at the PTA meeting.

◆

Smoke a cigar inside the public library.

Be the TV spokesperson for a new denture adhesive.

WHAT'S MY LINE?

Visit your teen at his first job serving hamburgers.

♦

Ask for free samples.

♦

Remark how cute he looks in his uniform.

♦

Tell the other customers he's your son.

♦

Call your daughter every half-hour when she's babysitting
to make sure everything's all right.

♦

Drop by to play with the baby.

♦

Get a job at your teen's school—be visible!

Help your teens with their paper route.

◆

Harass customers who don't pay.

◆

Bring your ferocious pit bull along when
you make collections.

◆

Run for public office on an education platform.

◆

Campaign for a twelve-month school year.

◆

Win the election.

◆

Have a job like "computer specialist" that defies
description.

◆

Become a sex therapist.

◆

Lose your job and have the word get around.

Open an obedience/boarding school for dogs.

◆

Be the town minister or psychotherapist.

◆

Become a professional wrestler.

◆

Appear in an ad for Preparation H.

◆

Be a modeling agent for your teenager. Book her for a
Clearasil commercial.

Serve liver and onions when your child has friends over for dinner.

YOU ARE WHAT YOU EAT

Add oat bran to every recipe in your collection.

◆

Substitute tofu for meat in all your recipes.

◆

Pack well-balanced, nutritious school lunches.

◆

Include pita bread with tofu and alfalfa sprouts, V-8, and dried prunes.

◆

Ask anyone at a fast food restaurant, "Are you sure you should be eating that?"

◆

Help yourself to food on your child's plate without being invited.

Make your famous Broccoli-Beet Surprise for the class party.

◆

Send store-bought cookies for the class party.

◆

Contribute a "Hamburger Helper" recipe to the school cookbook.

◆

Cut your child's sandwiches into cute shapes.

◆

Offer your teen's friends food every five minutes.

◆

Tell everyone your daughter ate dog food when she was a baby.

◆

Load up your plate and ask for a doggie bag when the family goes to an all-you-can-eat buffet.

◆

Ask your teens if they've washed their hands when they come to the dinner table.

Serve your bumper crop of carrots at every meal until the family turns orange.

◆

Keep leftovers in your refrigerator for years.

◆

Ask your teen if his science project on mold is causing the disgusting smell.

◆

Make a scene at the local Baskin-Robbins because they've discontinued peppermint fudge ribbon ice cream.

◆

Try to get a discount when you buy a year's supply of Girl Scout cookies.

Use a whistle to call the family together on outings.

ARE WE THERE YET?

Sing along with the car radio and forget the words.

◆

Make visiting cemeteries a high point of your vacation.

◆

Go on at length about how much you "love car trips!"

◆

Get carsick.

◆

Make frequent restroom stops.

◆

Insist that your child go bird-watching with the family.

◆

Make your child pose for a photo at every
tourist attraction.

Ask Mickey, Donald, and Goofy to pose for pictures with your teen at Disneyland.

◆

Buy souvenir T-shirts from every city you visit and expect your teens to wear them.

◆

Drive 20 miles per hour in a 55 miles-per-hour zone.

◆

Drive 80 miles per hour in a 35 miles-per-hour zone.

◆

Forget the airline tickets after rushing the whole family to the airport.

◆

Set off the airport security alarm with your Elvis Presley belt buckle.

◆

Arrange lodging for your family in a Paris brothel when your high school French fails you.

◆

Distract customs officials with your leopard-skin lingerie to hide the edelweiss you picked in the Alps.

Show your daughter's passport photo to the cute
tour guide.

◆

Take a wrong turn, get lost, and refuse to ask
for directions.

◆

Mimic the monkeys when you take the family to the zoo.

Show your son's date his messy room.

BACK AT THE RANCH

Put a "rap" message on the family's answering machine.

◆

Refuse to have a TV.

◆

Be the only family on your block to curbside recycle.

◆

Be the only family on your block *not* to curbside recycle.

◆

Have houseplants that die.

◆

Have a green thumb, and a living room that looks
like a jungle.

Put doilies on all the furniture.

◆

Put plastic covers on all your upholstered furniture.

◆

Rope off the living room so it won't get dirty.

◆

Use your son's ragged old jockey shorts for a dustcloth.

◆

Install a doorbell that plays "Home on the Range."

◆

Keep the ironing board in the living room.

◆

Move your kids into a shared room so you have a place for your dollhouse collection.

◆

Sing and play "air guitar" while cleaning the house.

◆

Invite your child's teacher over for dinner.

◆

Correct the teacher's grammar.

Bring out the baby pictures.

◆

Show everyone the bathtub shots.

◆

Hire a babysitter for your teens.

◆

Have a welcome mat that reads "Go Away."

Ask your teen if she sprayed when she returns from a trip to the bathroom.

GETTING PERSONAL

Be seen shopping in Victoria's Secret.

◆

Place an ad in the personals that describes you as "svelte,"
"sexy," or "fetching."

◆

Have a love life.

◆

Talk about your love life within earshot of your teens.

◆

Subscribe to *Playboy*.

◆

Subscribe to *Playgirl*.

◆

Read your teen's diary.

Talk to your teen's friends.

◆

Be sure to ask personal questions.

◆

Store your birth control pills in the medicine cabinet.

◆

Send your daughter to the store for sanitary napkins.

◆

Send your son to the store for sanitary napkins.

◆

Answer the doctor's questions about your teens instead of letting them respond.

◆

Be ten years older than everyone else's parents.

◆

Be ten years younger than everyone else's parents.

◆

Become a surrogate mother.

Hang your pantyhose to dry in the main bathroom.

◆

Frolic in the backyard hot tub.

◆

Kiss your spouse in public.

◆

Dedicate a love song to your spouse on your teen's
favorite radio station.

Arrive at school with the jockstrap your son forgot just as he's gotten the nerve to speak to the girl of his dreams.

FATAL ATTRACTION

Tell the class hunk's mother your daughter thinks
he's cute.

◆

Tell the mother of your son's secret flame that he's too shy
to ask out her daughter.

◆

Ask your teen's teacher out on a date.

◆

Suggest a boy or a girl your teen might "like like."

◆

Pick the class nerd as your number one choice.

◆

Run into your daughter's new heartthrob when you
haven't shaved all weekend.

Use a timer with a gong to limit your teen's phone calls.

◆

Flirt with anyone of the opposite sex.

◆

Be best friends with the school nerd's mother.

◆

Tell your daughter's best friend that she has a crush on the captain of the chess team.

◆

Take your teens to Single Parents Week at Club Med, and meet Mr. Right.

◆

Try to convince your teens to hang out with his teens.

◆

Turn around and stare at the girl your son is crazy about, after he *just* tells you not to look.

◆

Tell your son you're going to call the police after you get ten anonymous phone calls for him from girls.

Tell your daughter's new flame that she's in the bathroom.

◆

Forget to ask the name of the boy who called your daughter when she was out.

◆

Arrange a blind date for your teen.

◆

Tell all your friends the juicy details of your daughter's date.

Topple the display of bathroom tissue at the drugstore
because the color you want is on the bottom.

AT THE MALL

Run into your teen by accident when both of you are at
the mall with friends.

◆

Sit down and play "Chopsticks" on the demonstration
piano at the shopping center.

◆

Go to the mall with curlers in your hair.

◆

Push all pull doors, and pull all push doors.

◆

Come into the dressing room when your teen is
trying on clothes.

◆

Pick out all the wrong things for your teen to try on.

Comment freely on how the clothes look:

"That's a little tight around the hips."
"Isn't that a little long?"
"You look just like your father in that suit!"

◆

Drag your daughter to a discount clothing store where she must change in a common dressing room.

◆

Take your daughter shopping for a bra.

◆

Ask the salesclerk to help with the bra fitting.

◆

Take your son shopping for a jockstrap.

◆

Chew out the salesclerk for not knowing her stock.

◆

Make your teen guard the dressing room door when you're trying on bathing suits.

◆

Order your meal in Spanish at Taco Bell.

Perch on a flagpole at the mall until local deejays agree to ban heavy metal.

◆

Wear a sequined dress when you shop for groceries.

◆

Have more than ten items at the supermarket express line.

◆

Get stuck in a revolving door.

◆

Cut into the long line at the movies.

◆

Have your credit card refused because you're over the limit.

Lead the PTA's effort to patrol the halls at school.

THE THREE R'S

Drop your kids off at school.

◆

Be sure to kiss them good-bye.

◆

Pick your kids up at school.

◆

Be sure to honk the horn to announce your arrival.

◆

Go on a school trip.

◆

Enjoy the school trip, and say so.

◆

Refuse to go on the school trip.

Chaperone a school dance.

◆

Dance with another chaperone at the school dance.

◆

Dance with the principal at the school dance.

◆

Dance with a student at the school dance.

◆

Be your community's leading advocate for sex education in the schools.

◆

Take your campaign to your teen's school and have a rally there.

◆

Hand out condoms or "Just Say No" buttons on the school steps.

◆

Be interviewed by the local media and insist on bringing your family "on stage."

Bring bran muffins for your teen's class to snack on during the train trip to Chicago.

◆

Forget to turn your headlights off on graduation night, and have the principal page you from the podium.

◆

Give your teen driving lessons in the high school parking lot.

◆

Argue with the journalism teacher about why your teen wasn't selected as editor of the school paper.

Stay up late when your teens have slumber parties.

THE SOCIAL WHIRL

Host your niece's bachelorette party at Chippendale's.

◆

Have a mud-wrestling team as entertainment for your
fortieth birthday party.

◆

Drive your teens to their parties.

◆

Go in to the parties to see if parents are there.

◆

If they are, stay to talk with them.

◆

If they aren't, take your teens home.

◆

Dance the polka at the neighborhood block party.

Make your teens take along younger siblings when
going out with friends.

◆

Wake your teen's classmates with your snoring when
you chaperone the ski trip.

◆

Complain loudly about the service when eating out
with your kids.

◆

Send back your steak because it's too rare.

◆

Insist that the waiter reheat your teen's dinner.

◆

Act overly friendly with the waitress.

◆

Tell the busboy your daughter wants his phone number.

◆

When tasting wine, swish it around loudly in your
mouth and roll your eyes.

◆

Refuse the wine you have tasted.

Leave lipstick on your coffee cup.

◆

Blot your lipstick on a cloth napkin.

◆

Speak Chinese to the proprietor at your local
Hunan restaurant.

◆

Send compliments to the chef in a loud voice at your
neighborhood diner.

Walk out of a public restroom trailing toilet paper from your shoe.

WE'RE ONLY HUMAN

Sneeze loudly whenever you can.

◆

Have frequent coughing fits, especially during conferences
with your child's teachers.

◆

Be a hypochondriac.

◆

Pick up every germ that comes around.

◆

Burp.

◆

Burp in public.

◆

Have that other involuntary reaction.

Let your dandruff get out of control.

◆

Tell the dentist your child never flosses.

◆

Tell the dentist your child keeps the candy
store in business.

◆

Have world-class bad breath.

◆

Lock a spider in the bathroom because you can't
stand to kill it.

◆

Capture crickets under glass and make your child free
them outside when she comes home from school.

◆

Walk around with a pacifier in your mouth to help
break your cigarette habit.

◆

Practice CPR on the inflatable woman you got for
your fortieth birthday.

Walk into your teen's room without knocking.

◆

Call all your kids' names before you get to the one
you want.

◆

Catch the chicken pox and give it to your child.

◆

Forget where you put your glasses until your child says
they're on your face.

◆

Use Magic Sunless Tanning Creme and turn orange.

◆

Shout profanities at the driver who steals
your parking space.

Line your sidewalk with plastic tulips.

CHECKING OUT THE COMPETITION

Remind your teen that his older sister won the
ninth grade French prize.

◆

Compare your teen's PSAT scores with everyone else's.

◆

Enter a wet T-shirt contest.

◆

Enter your daughter in a Junior Miss pageant.

◆

Make your house look like a gingerbread castle by getting
carried away with the outside Christmas lights.

◆

Shape your hedges to look like Snow White and
the Seven Dwarfs.

Strong-arm the neighbors into buying magazine subscriptions so your daughter's class can win the prize.

◆

Do "Stupid Pet Tricks" on "Late Night with David Letterman."

◆

Enter a hog-calling contest.

◆

Take up bodybuilding and enter competitions.

◆

Correct your teen's teacher about Civil War facts and be proven wrong.

◆

Open your teen's SAT results as soon as they arrive.

◆

Monopolize the Nintendo.

◆

Hog the remote control and keep switching TV channels.

◆

Get to the bake-off finals and have your cake fall flat.

Install a windmill in your front yard to use as an alternative source of energy.

◆

Push your teen to the front of the pack when the bride's bouquet is being thrown.

◆

Call up the college admissions office to see if your teen has been accepted.

◆

Insist on running your teen's campaign for student body president.

Be a Star Trek groupie.

BRING ON THE CLOWNS

Sit in the first row at your child's glee club concert.

◆

Take lots of flash photos at the concert.

◆

Be sure to stand up, walk down the aisle, and otherwise
call attention to yourself.

◆

Present flowers to your child after the performance.

◆

Don't present flowers to your child after the performance.

◆

Go out for a post-performance treat, and sit next to
your child's teachers.

At the band concert, start clapping before the
piece is over.

◆

Videotape your son's debut as a heavy metal guitarist in
the school talent show.

◆

Sing along with the performers, preferably off-key.

◆

Tell jokes and forget the punch lines.

◆

Insist that your teen play "London Bridge" on the piano for
your friends.

◆

Dance along with Madonna on MTV.

◆

Swoon to Johnny Mathis.

◆

Start taking tuba lessons.

◆

Tell the same story over and over again.

Appear on "Star Search" as a stand-up comic and use your teens for material.

♦

Set up your fortune-telling booth at the Village Square Festival.

♦

Make your son wear a sandwich board to advertise your "Olde English Tea Room."

♦

Volunteer to be the subject of a hypnosis demonstration for the Y teens, and snore when you're put to sleep.

Get stuck in an intricate yoga position while demonstrating techniques to your daughter's Girl Scout troop.

THE SPORTING LIFE

Fall down as you try to hold on to the bunny hill rope tow.

◆

Be terrified at the top of the ski lift and ride it back to the bottom.

◆

Spend all day in the ski lodge because you forgot your long underwear.

◆

Lose your bikini top in the surf.

◆

Make a family of snowpeople in your front yard.

◆

Loot your teens' closets to clothe your snowfriends.

Bean the principal when you play in the
PTA golf tournament.

◆

Cheat when you can't get through the windmill on the
miniature golf course.

◆

Lose control of your horse and fall off during a trail ride.

◆

Chase your teen around the backyard with a squirt gun.

◆

Be an avid baseball fan, and have the lingo to prove it.

◆

Ride your ten-speed bike to work.

◆

Wear a thong bathing suit at the community pool.

◆

Sign up for belly-dancing classes.

◆

Run the wrong way when you play touch football with the
neighborhood kids.

Try out your teen's new Rollerblades and break your leg.

◆

Go for a dunk shot while playing basketball with your teen and rip the backboard off the garage.

◆

Paint your car the colors of your favorite NFL team.

◆

Black out your front teeth when you take your son and his friends to the hockey game.

Put reindeer antlers on your poodle for the holidays.

LOVE ME, LOVE MY PET

Walk the dog while still in your bathrobe.

◆

Put a collar with blinking lights on your Saint Bernard.

◆

Teach your pet parrot to wolf-whistle.

◆

Keep a goat to eat the grass so you won't have to mow it.

◆

Dress your poodle in a plaid doggie sweater and ribbons
and walk it around the block.

◆

Call her "precious" when she strays or dawdles.

◆

Let your dog run loose in the neighborhood.

Cook special soups and stews for your cocker spaniel.

◆

Let your bird fly loose in the house.

◆

Keep an ant farm.

◆

Do birdcalls on your local TV station's talent show.

◆

Feed spaghetti to your dog, strand by strand.

◆

Build a canopy bed for your Persian cat.

◆

Put costumes on your pets for Halloween.

◆

Name the plastic flamingos who live in your front yard.

◆

Have a birthday party for your pet, and invite all the cats
and dogs in the neighborhood.

Sneak your dog into your hotel while on a family vacation.

◆

Paper the den in jungle prints so your pet boa will
feel at home.

◆

Use the stack of newspapers your teen was saving for a
report to paper-train the new puppy.

Drive an old car that backfires.

THE WHOLE
TOWN'S TALKING

Leave the Christmas tree up until March.

◆

Sing like Pavarotti while you trim the hedges.

◆

Feature your teen's baby clothes and toys at the
neighborhood yard sale.

◆

Use your child's pet name in public.

◆

Talk like a Valley Girl.

◆

Use outdated words and phrases, such as "jeepers,"
"guffaw," "I dare say," and "chat."

Call "Dinner's ready!" from the kitchen window.

◆

Call "There's a girl on the phone!" to your son down the block.

◆

Call "There's a boy on the phone!" to your daughter across the street.

◆

Get a fit of the giggles during parents' Sex Ed Night.

◆

Accompany your teen to a rock concert.

◆

Wear your ear plugs.

◆

Make your teen wear ear plugs.

◆

Try to hold your teen's hand when crossing a busy street.

◆

Include your son's letters to Santa Claus in the time capsule being buried in the town square.

Change your hair color. . .often.

◆

Be mentioned in the gossip column of your
local newspaper.

◆

Get a facelift.

◆

Get a hair transplant.

◆

Reek of cheap perfume.

Make your teen's teacher a needlepoint pillow that says
"World's Greatest Teacher."

SUCKING UP AT SCHOOL

Defend any of your son's teachers in front of his friends.

◆

Brag to your teen's calculus teacher that you
majored in math.

◆

Tell your teen's geometry teacher that you flunked
geometry and still don't get it.

◆

Touch the oil paintings at the museum on your child's
art class field trip.

◆

Get a reprimand from the museum guard for touching
the artwork.

◆

Offer to show your child's band director your technique
on the trumpet.

Volunteer to run the school library and nag students who don't return books on time.

◆

Give recycled fruit cake as holiday gifts to teachers.

◆

Initiate a Teacher Appreciation Luncheon for the faculty.

◆

Volunteer your teen and friends to clean up after school football games.

◆

Sign up to talk about your job on Career Day.

◆

Contribute your membership in Pound Punchers to the school auction after your diet goes awry.

◆

Attend after-school Latin Club meetings to brush up on your language skills.

◆

Serve as a judge at the Science Fair.

Write, direct, and star in the PTA's annual musical.

◆

Flirt with your teen's chemistry teacher.

◆

Demonstrate an old high school cheer to
your teen's friends.

◆

Arrive late at the school play and say "Excuse me" to
each person in your row.

◆

Clip your fingernails during the play.

Host "Ballroom Dancing for Teens" on a local cable TV channel.

HOORAY FOR HOLLYWOOD!

Sit behind your son and his date at the movies.

◆

Offer to share your popcorn with them.

◆

Talk loudly throughout the show.

◆

Cover your son's eyes during the sex scenes.

◆

Have your pager beep during a tender love scene.

◆

Sit at the end of the row and refuse to stand up when other people need to leave.

Sit in the middle of the row and climb over everyone to get to the snack bar.

◆

Do this often, and spill popcorn on everyone as you return.

◆

Put the fake Oscar you bought at Universal Studios on the mantel.

◆

Videotape your son's first shaving experience and submit it to "America's Funniest Home Videos."

◆

Tape your favorite soap over the video of your daughter's Olympic gymnastics trials.

◆

Insist that your teen demonstrate the waltz on a cable TV show.

◆

Use "Let Arthritis Be Your Guide" as your theme when you audition as weather forecaster for the local TV station.

Cry at the sad parts when you see rental movies with
your child and his friends.

◆

Be the only parents who forbid their teen to see
Stephen King's latest thriller.

◆

Be the only parents who take their teen to see
Stephen King's latest thriller.

◆

Play Gypsy Rose Lee in a community theater production.

◆

Try out for "Family Feud."

◆

Offer your services as Arnold Schwarzenegger's
bodyguard when he comes to town to film
Gulliver's Travels.

Entertain your daughter's date with card tricks while she finishes dressing.

BE HOME BY 11

Interview your daughter's first date.

◆

Grill him about his past, present, and future.

◆

Make sure he knows you expect his intentions to
be honorable.

◆

Open the big red envelope that arrives for your son on
February 14.

◆

Recognize your daughter's admirer by name when
he calls.

◆

Don't recognize him; ask "Who's calling?"

Hug your daughter's first date when he appears
at your door.

◆

Shake hands with him instead.

◆

Regale your teen's date with tales of your
high school escapades.

◆

Ask your daughter's date to help you rearrange the
living room furniture.

◆

Eavesdrop on your son's five-hour-long phone call.

◆

Bring up last week's heartthrob after it's all over.

◆

Call your teen's date by the wrong name.

◆

Realize that you forgot to mail your son's letter to
his girlfriend.

◆

Insist on taking photos of your daughter and her date
before they leave.

Park under a pigeon roost just before your son is going to use the car for his first date.

◆

Turn on the porch light just as your daughter and her date walk up to the door.

◆

Use the rearview mirror to spy on your son and his date in the backseat when you chauffeur them to the movies.

◆

Ask your daughter's date to show you his license before you'll let her get in his car.

Greet your teen with balloons as the school bus returns
from a weekend tournament.

YOU CAN DO IT!

Chew out the ref for a bad call at the school
basketball game.

◆

Put a "Welcome Home" banner across the front of your
house when your child comes home from camp.

◆

Tell the soccer team that your son's imaginary friend
taught him how to kick.

◆

Break the principal's window when you hit a homer at
the class picnic.

◆

Shrink your son's football jersey right before
the big game.

◆

Drop the baton in the father-son relay race.

Bounce your bowling ball down the gutter on
Family Bowling Night.

◆

Hit the refreshment stand with your bowling ball when
it rolls backwards.

◆

Ask which team is wearing the maroon and gold jerseys
during the Super Bowl.

◆

Split your pants while bending over to field a grounder at
the faculty/parent softball game.

◆

Then strike out in the bottom of the ninth with
the bases loaded.

◆

Rush up and hug your teen when she wins the swim meet.

◆

Sing "Row, Row, Row Your Boat" from the shore as your
teen's crew team strokes by.

◆

Insist that "XEBEC" is really a word when you get a triple-
letter score while playing in the local Scrabble tournament.

Plead with your teen to let you join his weekend war games club.

◆

Bore the geography bee finalists with a lecture on your travels around the world.

◆

Collide with the minister while launching your kite at the spring charity tournament.

◆

Try to jump the net à la Jimmy Connors when you and your child win a doubles match, and fall flat on your face.

◆

Lie about the one that got away when you return empty-handed from the company fishing excursion.

◆

Challenge your son's friends to an arm-wrestling match.

Start to pull out of the gas station while the hose is still in your gas tank.

IT BEATS WALKING

Meet the school bus with milk and cookies.

◆

Meet the school bus in your robe and slippers.

◆

Get stopped for speeding while driving the car pool.

◆

Get stopped for driving 20 miles per hour when the speed limit is 65.

◆

Insist on listening to the classical music station when you drive your son and his friends to the mall.

◆

Put "MOM TAXI" on your vanity tags.

Have a bumper sticker that says "Insanity is inherited; you get it from your kids."

◆

Hit a parked car as you demonstrate the fine art of parallel parking to your teen.

◆

Threaten to throw kids out of the car pool if they don't stop kicking the back of your seat.

◆

Use your bowling trophy as a hood ornament.

◆

Strap an artificial flower to your car antenna.

◆

Protect your teen with your arm whenever you brake.

◆

Hang pine forest air freshener from the rearview mirror.

◆

Run out of gas while driving the cast to opening night of the spring drama production.

◆

Install beaded backrests on all the seats in your car.

Strap on a safety helmet when you help your son practice for his driving test.

◆

Make a sun shield for your car that proclaims "Happy Family Travels Here!"

◆

Get a flat on your way to the ninth grade formal, and ask your daughter's date to help you fix it.

◆

Offer the principal a lift home.

◆

Burn rubber when you leave the school parking lot.

◆

Go through a red light on the same trip.

Seat your teens at the kiddie table on Thanksgiving and at other family gatherings.

WE'LL ONLY STAY AN HOUR

Drag your child to family reunions.

◆

Agree with Aunt Ethel about "how big he's grown!"

◆

Point out to Cousin Jasper that "he's got his
daddy's skinny legs!"

◆

Ask your daughter if she remembers Great Uncle Billy,
who last saw her when she was two.

◆

While watching the Grammys, ask your teen and his
cousins, "So who's this guy, Hammer?"

◆

Insist that your child come along to your uncle's retirement
party in Buffalo and get snowed in for a week.

Prompt your teen to say "Thank you" when given a gift.

◆

Give your child a name that everyone mispronounces.

◆

Be an outcast at your family reunion picnic when gnats swarm to your hair spray.

◆

Offer your daughter's services as a babysitter at her aunt's wedding.

◆

Make your son slow-dance with Great Aunt Mabel at her eightieth birthday party.

◆

Elbow your son when he dozes off during the ninety-fifth retelling of Grandpa's war stories.

◆

Force your daughter to go to the movies with the cousin she hates.

◆

Reserve front-row seats for your family at the Tiny Tots Violin Recital in which your nephew has a solo.

Rent matching plaid dinner jackets for you and your son to wear to Grandma and Grandpa's fiftieth wedding anniversary party.

◆

Knock over the wedding cake while teaching your daughter to jitterbug at Aunt Susan's reception.

◆

Get caught skinny-dipping in the lake.

◆

Hook a ringer on the fence post after predicting you'll win the family horseshoes tournament.

◆

Ask your daughter to take Grandma to the restroom.

Make mobiles out of wire coat hangers and Brillo to sell at the school fund-raiser.

FOR FUN AND PROFIT

Sign up to teach an after-school class in growing
zucchini—your specialty.

◆

Hang your velvet Elvis painting over the mantel.

◆

Make your son wear your engineer's hat when he
runs your model trains.

◆

Go on "Oprah" to discuss your previous lives as Cleopatra,
Marie Antoinette, and a rutabaga farmer from Dubuque.

◆

Raid your neighbors' trash piles and sell your discoveries
at the flea market.

◆

Start an ostrich farm.

Make earrings out of twist ties, and wear them.

◆

Fashion art objects out of dryer lint and display them
at the public library.

◆

Use leftover wallpaper to wrap gifts.

◆

Recycle gift wrap.

◆

Become a mime and use Main Street as your stage.

◆

Present your teen's French teacher with a Q-tip sculpture
of the Eiffel Tower for Napoleon's Birthday.

◆

Make refrigerator magnets out of your
teen's baby pictures.

◆

Collect cuckoo clocks and display them all over the house.

◆

Submit your paint-by-number artwork to the
Women's League art show.

Make your son wear an apron when he helps you make dinner.

◆

Teach your teen's friends how to do the Twist.

◆

Show your teen and his pals how to twirl three hula hoops at once.

Hold a family funeral for the pet goldfish that died.

BELIEVE IT OR NOT

Claim you've sighted Elvis.

♦

Refuse to drive the car pool on Friday the 13th.

♦

Bring out your tarot cards at every family gathering.

♦

Consult a psychic.

♦

Have an astrologer plot your family's astrological charts.

♦

Go into business as a palm reader.

♦

Become a channeler so you can speak for a 2,500-year-old wise man.

Paint good luck charms on the front of your house to ward off evil spirits.

◆

Join a motorcycle gang.

◆

Call a talk show to discuss your kidnapping by aliens.

◆

Fall asleep during the minister's sermon and snore loudly.

◆

Make change from the collection plate.

◆

Spill the collection plate.

◆

Keep singing "Rock of Ages" after the rest of the congregation has finished.

◆

Buttonhole the preacher on the church steps as a long line forms to talk with him.

Claim that Jimmy Hoffa visited your seance.

◆

Join a witches coven.

◆

Be on speaking terms with the ghost who lives in the attic.

◆

Insist on watching Lawrence Welk reruns.

Argue with the guy at the carnival midway that his game is fixed when you don't win a teddy bear.

YOU'RE A WINNER!

Enter every contest that comes along.

◆

Announce that you've won a sweepstakes, and then find out the prize is worth 40¢.

◆

Drive 400 miles to buy lottery tickets in another state.

◆

Tell your teens what you'll buy them from your lottery winnings (when you win).

◆

Tell your family over breakfast that Ed McMahon visited you in your dreams and awarded you $10 million.

◆

Have a major fight with your spouse over the color Jaguar you'll win.

Head for the coupon inserts with your scissors as soon as the Sunday paper arrives.

◆

Plan your menu around the coupons that expire that week.

◆

Serve your family lima bean stew just because you had a coupon for it (even though everyone hates lima beans).

◆

Take over the rec room with the box tops, bottle caps, and UPC symbols you're saving for rebates and refunds.

◆

Buy the gallon-size bottle of tabasco sauce to save money per ounce.

◆

Enter your teen's photo in Clearasil's Man of the Month poster contest.

◆

Ask your son to escort you to the final round of the Chamber of Commerce Super Mom competition.

Rip the felt on the pool table with your cue after you've challenged your daughter and friends to a game.

◆

Win a drawing to have your bunion surgery featured on the medical cable channel.

◆

Lose your blue-ribbon pie when your pet hog gets too close to the bakery table at the county fair.

◆

Receive only three votes when you run for City Council.

◆

Win a family trip to Mexico and discover it involves pitching a tent on the beach.

◆

Win the drawing to sink baskets at half-time when the Lakers come to town, and miss every one.

◆

Redeem your free Feline Feast coupons because you might get a cat someday and can't resist a bargain.

Super-Glue your son to his science project when you offer to help.

DO IT YOURSELF

Find out how few buckets you have when the roof you repaired springs leaks every six inches.

◆

Spend twelve hours hanging your new front door and then be unable to close it.

◆

Fill the rec room with lint when the dryer vent you installed doesn't quite work.

◆

Use orange crates to decorate your guest room.

◆

Put off fixing the leak in the upstairs bathroom until the ceiling falls in on your teen's Sweet Sixteen party.

◆

Set up your radial saw in the living room.

Tell your teen that nobody will notice if the pattern in the wallpaper you're hanging in her bedroom doesn't match.

◆

Take down the dead tree in your backyard and the back of your house along with it.

◆

Rip off the wallpaper in the front hall before you're ready to replace it.

◆

Astro-turf your yard to cut down on the mowing.

◆

Rewire your toaster and then watch it catch fire the first time you use it.

◆

Build a boat in your basement and be unable to get it out.

◆

Refuse to cut off tags on pillows that say "DO NOT REMOVE UNDER PENALTY OF LAW."

◆

Turn all your son's underwear pink by washing it with your red sweatshirt.

Recycle your daughter's old bed sheets as curtains for the new rec room.

◆

Wake up the neighborhood with your leaf blower at the crack of dawn.

◆

Promise your teen that a Band-Aid will hold up the hem of her cheerleading skirt.

◆

Install a pay phone in your entry hall.

◆

Offer to make your daughter's prom dress to save money.

Give your daughter a home perm that makes her look as if she stuck her finger in a light socket.

THE BODY IMPERFECT

Come downstairs in your underwear just as your teen's friends have arrived to work on the history project.

◆

"Adjust" your child's carefully fixed hair.

◆

Clean a smudge off your child's face with a licked handkerchief.

◆

Make your teen wear a garlic necklace during flu season.

◆

Chew bubble gum and blow bubbles.

◆

Take out your dentures whenever they bother you.

Gesture wildly when making a point to your teen.

◆

Go to a witch doctor to cure your dandruff.

◆

Imitate Cher and get a tattoo.

◆

Be a klutz and trip over everything.

◆

Tell your teen's friend he has lettuce in his braces.

◆

Shave your head and find it's not the shape to shave.

◆

Join your daughter at the gym and have hair on your legs
long enough to braid.

◆

Use your gargling as an alarm to wake the swim team
when they sleep over before a meet.

◆

Belt out "New York, New York" while you lather
up in the shower.

Put up a see-through shower curtain in your
teen's bathroom.

◆

Always be early.

◆

Always be late.

◆

Look like a Barbie doll after your makeover at the
cosmetics counter.

Give your future daughter-in-law *The Joy of Sex* at
her bridal shower.

YOU'RE NEVER TOO OLD

Tell your son's fiancée that he sucked his thumb until
he was ten.

◆

Make sure he's there to confirm the report.

◆

Let your grandchildren know about the time their mommy
cut off her pigtails with her plastic scissors.

◆

Tell your son's business partner about his favorite stuffed
animal, Woof-Woof.

◆

Have your daughter paged at her law firm, making sure
the announcement says her mother is calling.

◆

Consult a matchmaker to find a husband for
your daughter.

Respond to ads seeking "tall, dark, and handsome" men to
see if the advertisers are worthy of your son.

◆

Weep when you leave your daughter at college.

◆

Attend the same college where your son or daughter
is enrolled.

◆

Take the same classes.

◆

Make straight As.

◆

Sob hysterically at your son's wedding.

◆

Show off your daughter's engagement ring to
all your friends.

◆

Tell your son's in-laws how lucky they are to have
him in the family.

◆

Ask your married child, "When are we going to have
grandchildren?"

Lie about your age.

◆

Display your college student's seventh grade picture over the fireplace.

◆

Refuse to speak to your son's mother-in-law because you think she snubbed you at a party.

◆

Call your daughter's employer to say she deserves a raise.

◆

Include copies of your unborn grandchild's sonogram with the Christmas cards you send.

Tell "When I was your age. . ." stories in front of
your teen's friends.

DOWN TO BASICS

Exist.

◆

Be right.

◆

Be wrong.

◆

Suggest anything.

◆

Point out that your suggestions are usually
followed. . .eventually.

◆

Scold or ground your son in front of his friends.

◆

Talk to everyone you meet as if you've known
them all your life.

Tell jokes.

◆

Tell bad jokes.

◆

Tell dumb jokes.

◆

Tell ethnic jokes.

◆

Crack your gum.

◆

Slurp your soup.

◆

Pick your teeth.

◆

Lick an envelope.

◆

Put on lipstick in public.

◆

Speak loudly in public.

Laugh in public.

◆

Speak to your teen in public.

◆

Kiss your teen in public.

◆

Say "I love you" to your teen in public.

◆

Write this book.

◆

Sign your name to this book.

◆

Dedicate this book to the children you've embarrassed.

"I Embarrass My Kids Without Even Trying" Button

You're going to embarrass your kids—you can't avoid it. So why not be proud of it, and wear this button?

Order #4006

2¼ inch metal button

"I Drive My Parents Crazy Without Even Trying" Button

Parents embarrass you, and you're too young to do much about it. Or are you? Here's the perfect way to show your parents that two can play this game.

Order #4007

2¼ inch metal button

Dads Say the Dumbest Things!

by Bruce Lansky and K.L. Jones

Lansky and Jones have collected all the greatest lines dads have ever used to get kids to stop fighting in the car, feed the pet, turn off the TV while doing their homework, and get home before curfew. It includes such winners as: "What do you want a pet for—you've got a sister" and "When I said 'feed the goldfish,' I didn't mean feed them to the cat." A fun gift for dad.

Order #4220

Moms Say the Funniest Things!

by Bruce Lansky

Bruce Lansky has collected all the greatest lines moms have ever used to deal with "emergencies" like getting the kids out of bed in the morning, cleaned, dressed, to school, to the dinner table, undressed, and back to bed. It includes such all-time winners as: "Put on clean underwear—you never know when you'll be in an accident" and "If God had wanted you to fool around, He would have written the 'Ten Suggestions.'" A fun gift for mom.

Order #4280

Order Form

Qty.	Title	Author	Order No.	Unit Cost	Total
	Best Baby Shower Book, The	Cooke, C.	1239	$6.00	
	Best Party Book,The	Warner, P.	6089	$7.00	
	Best Wedding Shower Book, The	Cooke, C.	6059	$6.00	
	Dads Say the Dumbest Things!	Lansky/Jones	4220	$6.00	
	David, We're Pregnant!	Johnston, L.	1049	$6.00	
	Do They Ever Grow Up?	Johnston, L.	1089	$6.00	
	Grandma Knows Best	McBride, M.	4009	$5.00	
	Hi, Mom! Hi, Dad!	Johnston, L.	1139	$6.00	
	How to Embarrass Your Kids	Holleman/Sherins	4005	$6.00	
	How to Outsmart Your Kids	Dodds, B.	4190	$5.00	
	How to Survive 40th Birthday	Dodds, B.	4260	$6.00	
	Italian Without Words	Cangelosi/Carpini	5100	$4.95	
	Kids Pick the Funniest Poems	Lansky, B.	2410	$13.00	
	Moms Say the Funniest Things!	Lansky, B.	4280	$6.00	
	Mother Murphy's Law	Lansky, B.	1149	$4.50	
	Mother Murphy's 2nd Law	Lansky, B.	4010	$4.50	
	Unofficial College Dictionary	Cohen/Zweig	4170	$4.95	
	Wierd Wonders	Schreiber, B.	4120	$4.95	
	World's Funniest Roast Jokes	Stangland, R.	4030	$6.00	
	"I Drive My Parents Crazy Without Even Trying!" Button		4007	$1.00	
	"I Embarrass My Kids Without Even Trying!" Button		4006	$1.00	
				Subtotal	
			Shipping and Handling (see below)		
			MN residents add 6.5% sales tax		
				Total	

YES! Please send me the books indicated above. Add $2.00 shipping and handling for the first book and 50¢ for each additional book (no additional charges, however, for button orders). Add $2.50 to total for books shipped to Canada. Overseas postage will be billed. Allow up to 4 weeks for delivery. Send check or money order payable to Meadowbrook Press. No cash or C.O.D.'s, please. Prices subject to change without notice. **Quantity discounts available upon request.**

Send book(s) to:

Name _____ Address _____

City _____ State _____ Zip _____

Telephone (_____)_____ P.O. number (if necessary) _____

Payment via: ❑ Check or money order payable to Meadowbrook Press
(No cash or C.O.D.'s, please) Amount enclosed $ _____
❑ Visa (for orders over $10.00 only.) ❑ MasterCard (for orders over $10.00 only.)

Account # _____ Signature _____ Exp. Date _____

A _FREE_ Meadowbrook Press catalog is available upon request.
You can also phone us for orders of $10.00 or more at 1-800-338-2232.

Mail to: Meadowbrook, Inc.
                    18318 Minnetonka Boulevard, Deephaven, MN 55391
(612) 473-5400   Toll -Free 1-800-338-2232   Fax (612) 475-0736